Healthy Sports Poetry
The Secret Collection

Sem

Copyright

Copyright © 2023 Sem Duchateau All rights reserved

The characters and events portrayed in this book are fictitious. Any similarity to real persons, living or dead, is coincidental and not intended by the author.

ISBN: 9798851551635

Imprint: Independently published

No part of this book may be reproduced, or stored in a retrieval system, or transmitted in any form or by any means, electronic, mechanical, photocopying, recording, or otherwise, without express written permission of the publisher.

Dedicated to

Heidi the love of my life

Introduction

A Journey of Strength and Resilience: Exploring Health and Sports

In this book, we embark on a captivating journey into the intertwined worlds of health and sports. From the pulsating beats of a runner's heart to the strategic moves on a chessboard, we delve deep into the multifaceted connections between physical well-being, athletic pursuits, and the human spirit.

"A Journey of Strength and Resilience: Exploring Health and Sports" invites you to explore the diverse landscapes of health and sports, beyond the mere physicality. It is a collection of poetic musings.

You will encounter the boundless joys and challenges of sports, the impact of physical activities on mental well-being, and the triumphs and obstacles faced by athletes from all walks of life.
From the exhilarating rush of conquering a mountain peak to the quiet discipline of nurturing one's body and mind, this book is a testament to the transformative power of health and sports.

Content

- The right way and misconceptions — P. 7 - 9
- Losing weight and building muscle — P. 10 - 11
- Sports for honour or glittering height — P. 12 - 15
- Nations pride — P. 16 - 17
- Indoors or outdoors — P. 19 - 20
- Obsession — P. 21 - 24
- 'Depression' a Western privilege? — P. 25 - 26
- Our Sports and beliefs — P. 27 - 29
- Young and Old — P. 30 - 31
- Healing pain — P. 32 - 34
- Diet and sport — P. 35 - 36
- More on Diet and Sport — P. 37 - 38

More Content

- Free diving in the wild   P.39 - 40
- Rodeo   P.41 - 42
- King of sports 'Splash'   P.43 - 44
- Embrace the power of sport   P.45 - 46
- Chess as a Sport   P.47 - 48
- Genetics   P.49 - 50
- Discipline   P.51 - 52
- Sports for all   P.53 - 54
- Hydration   P.55 - 57
- Sport and Ethics   P.58 - 59
- Heroes and Legends   P.60 - 61
- Politics   P.62 - 63
- Crazy and entertaining   P.64 - 65
- Gambling   P.66 - 67
- Dope   P.68 - 69
- Eternity   P.70 - 73

The right way and misconceptions

In the rush of modern days, we chase after health's allure,
A society obsessed, consumed by a wellness cure. In gyms adorned with sleek machines, we strive for sculpted frames,
Dreams of strength and stamina, amidst societal claims.

The treadmill's steady hum echoes a ceaseless quest, For bodies that mirror, society's ideal manifest. But pause, my friend, take heed and see, Do we chase true health or just a mirage of glee?

We're told to sweat and strain, to push ourselves each day, Yet, is exercise a remedy, in every single way? Does the striving for perfection bring joy or cause dismay?
Are we nourishing our souls, or only our bodies in this play?

Don't mistake me, dear reader, for I know the joy it brings,

To feel your muscles stretch, as endorphins take their wings.
Sports can teach us discipline, teamwork, and the grace, To strive for greatness, to challenge ourselves, in every single race.

But let us not forget, in our quest for athletic might, That health is not defined by muscles, bulging and tight.
It dwells within the heart, the mind, in balance and in peace,
A state where body and spirit find a sweet, harmonious lease.

A marathon may grant you strength, yet leave your soul bereft,
If you neglect the simple joys, in your hurried quest to be deft.
For health encompasses more than treadmills and weights,
It's found in laughter, love, and moments of stillness, great.
So, embrace the sports and the sweat, but do it with a mind,
That values rest and self-care, for a life that's truly kind. For it's not in a gym or on a field, where health's secrets unfold,

But in the spaces between, where true well-being takes hold.

An elite baseball stadium

Losing weight and building muscle

In the pursuit of strength, in search of a fitter frame, We delve into the labyrinth, where health and sports lay claim. Whispers of weight loss echo in the halls, As we navigate the maze, deciphering what truly calls. The magazines tout secrets, promising the perfect shape, With plans and diets, formulas they eagerly drape. But beneath the glossy surface, let's seek a different view, Beyond the glitz and glamour, to what truly rings true.

For there's no magic potion, no shortcut to the goal, No single prescription that will make us whole.
To lose the weight, build muscle, we must first understand, The power of consistency, a dedication grand.

It's not about the latest trend or the numbers on a scale,

But the relationship we foster with our bodies, without fail. It's in the daily choices, the habits that we form, That we find the true essence, where health begins to swarm. Nourish with intention, savouring each bite, Embracing wholesome foods, the ones that feel just right.
Move with purpose, finding joy in every stride, Not as a chore, but as a celebration of life's ride.

For muscles grow through effort, in the push and pull we find, Strength in perseverance, in the resilience of the mind. So, let us honour our bodies, with compassion and with care, Embracing the journey, knowing transformation is rare.

Remember, dear seeker, it's a process, not a race, An array of choices, where patience finds its space. In losing weight and building muscle, let's not forget the grace, To love ourselves wholly, at every single pace.

Sports for honour or glittering height

In ages past, when wars did rage, Sports bore a different heritage,
A preparation for battle and might,
To survive in a world so fierce and tight.

In fields and arenas, the warriors stood,
Honed their skills for the greater good, A dance of combat, a measured art,
Where survival relied on strength and heart.

Their bodies trained for life's dire call, To protect their kin, to stand tall,
In mud and dust, they found their worth, In grit and sweat, they proved their birth.

But now, as centuries weave their tale, The meaning of sports starts to pale, A transformation, a shift profound,
In how they're cherished, how they're crowned.

Today's arena shines a different light, Money, fame, a glittering height, Society's illusions, appearances' sway, Bend the purpose, change the play. Athletes moulded into stars,
Their worth, a measure, not just in scars, The world demands a polished face, While core values find a hiding place.

But midst the glitz, let's not forget,
The heart of sports, the timeless bet, For in the essence, still resides,
The strength of spirit, where truth abides.

Beyond the fame, beyond the gold,
The lessons learned, both young and old, In sports, we find a mirror clear,
To strive, to push, to face our fear.

So, may we treasure the roots of yore, The primal need to fight and soar,
Yet seek to balance, to redefine,
What sports mean in this modern line.
For within each game, a chance to glean,
The human spirit's strength unseen,
To celebrate more than the show, And find in sports a deeper glow.

Indoors

Carrying water as a means of life

Nation's pride

In every corner of this spinning earth,
In lands of sun, of snow, of rugged mirth, A
tapestry of sports, a woven thread, Embodies
nations' pride, their spirit spread.

On Asian fields, where silence finds its grace,
In martial arts, where movement holds its place, A low
pace blooms, with discipline refined,
A dance of souls, a treasure to find.

In Europe's heart, where passion burns like fire, In football's
fervour, a nation's true desire,
With every kick, a heartbeat's thump, Unifying
voices, a collective jump.

From Africa's plains, where runners speed, In the
marathons, a rhythm to heed, Endurance tested,
strength of will,
A testament to life's unyielding thrill.

In South America's sun-kissed embrace, On
football fields, where skills embrace, A samba
of feet, a carnival of pride,
A symphony of colours, where dreams collide.

North America, too, finds its way,
On icy rinks, where hockey's players sway, In brutal

grace, they glide and fight,
A symbol of strength, of national might.

In Oceania's seas, where waves entwine, Surfers ride, a dance with the divine,
In harmony with ocean's raw embrace,
A connection profound, a love they chase.

Even in the odd, remote terrains,
Where danger lurks and life's at pains, The pride persists, in daring feats,
A testament to human spirits' heats.

From the icy heights to desert sand, In every nation, sports command,
A mirror to pride, to identity, To unify, to set the spirit free.

For in this world of varied hue,
In sports, we find a common view, A celebration of who we are,
In every stride, near and far.

Indoors or outdoors

In the sheltered walls, where echoes reverberate, Indoor sports find their silent, contained state, The controlled environment, a steady embrace, Where bodies move, seeking a rhythmic space.

The weight of the iron, the hush of the court, Within these walls, a different world is brought, Yet as we strive, with machines and routine,
Do we lose touch with nature's vibrant scene?

For outside, in open fields, a different story unfolds, Where sports take flight, as nature's secrets are beheld,
The air alive with whispers of trees and wind, As bodies stretch, nature's beauty begins.

Lungs expand, craving oxygen's sweet song, As feet meet earth, hearts begin to throng, The sun's gentle kiss, on skin and soul, Outdoor sports ignite a primal, spirited role.

For in the open spaces, where skies unfurl, We find the nourishment, that fuels the world, The boundless horizons, a canvas so grand,

Inspiring movement, from every muscle strand.

The rhythm of feet upon trails and tracks, The
rush of adrenaline, the wind at our backs,
Outdoor sports awaken our senses anew, With every
breath, nature's wonders accrue.

Indoors or outdoors, both hold their grace, But let
us not forget nature's wild embrace, For in her
arms, we find solace and might, A symbiotic dance, in
both day and night.

So, let us honour the walls that house our dreams, And seek the
freedom where nature gleams,
For in the balance of both, we come alive, The body,
the mind, the spirit will thrive.

With every breath, as lungs fill with air,
In sports, we find the essence of being aware, Of the
interconnectedness, that binds us all, Indoor or
outdoor, where our bodies enthral.

Obsession

In the hallowed arena, where dreams collide, A dark undercurrent flows, hard to hide, Obsession lurks, a treacherous guise,
A delusional tunnel, where sanity flies.

With every stride, a yearning for perfection, A relentless pursuit, a dangerous infection,
The mind entangled, consumed by the chase, As reality distorts, leaving no trace.

The body pushed beyond its own measure, An addiction to triumph, a perilous treasure, In the quest for greatness, a soul may sway, Lost in the shadows, where balance gives way.

For what is the cost of this relentless desire? When health is neglected, consumed by the fire,
When sports become shackles, an oppressive might, Devouring spirits, extinguishing light.

In the pursuit of glory, a twisted game, Where passion turns toxic, feeding the flame, The body a vessel, a pawn in the race,

While sanity wavers, leaving no space.

But let us not forget, amidst the haze,
That sports should uplift, inspire and amaze, A celebration of strength, of the human form, A

catalyst for growth, amidst the storm.

A reminder to temper the fervour within, To cherish the joy, the love sports bring, For health lies not only in victories won,
But in balance restored, when obsession is undone.

So tread with caution, in the realm of sport,
Nurture the body, the mind, and report, That wellness stems from a holistic view, Where sanity thrives and dreams renew.

Let us break free from the tunnel's deceptive lure, Embrace the essence of sports, sincere and pure, For in its truest form, a healing balm resides,
Where health and sports intertwine, life's symphony presides.

Jogging by the ocean

American football action

'Depression' a Western privilege?

In lands of privilege, where abundance thrives, The Western world dances, on fortunes' tides, In sports and health, a playground to explore, Yet unaware of the depths beyond their door.

For some, each day begins with a herculean task, A journey to school, an arduous ask,
Through treacherous paths, rough and steep, Where footsteps falter, and hearts may weep.

Others carry burdens, like water on their back, Miles upon miles, on a relentless track,
Their bodies ache, with every weary stride,
A testament to survival, where strength abides.

In the Western world, where desires hold sway, Depression lurks, an insidious display,
For even with plenty, it's never enough,
As the mind succumbs, to desires beyond one's stuff.

Easy access to gyms, to wellness, to care,
Yet the soul craves solace, beyond what's there, While in distant lands, where privilege is rare,

Richness resides, in the mind's heartfelt prayer.

For those without privilege, they find solace divine, In nature's embrace, in life's rhythmic line,
They see each day as a gift, a blessing untold, To live, to strive, to see another unfold.

In the Western world's abundance and ease,
May we pause and consider, the balance that frees, To cherish the blessings, to temper the wants,
And acknowledge the struggles, that life often flaunts.

For in the midst of privilege, let's not forget, The strength of the spirit, that others beget,
In physical challenges, they find resilience profound, God's provision of encouragement, all around.

So, as we pursue health and sports, let's be aware, Of the stark disparities, of life's uneven share,
May we strive for gratitude, with hearts open wide, For the privilege we hold, and the world's untamed stride.

Our Sports and beliefs

In the web of sports, beliefs intertwine,
A mosaic of faith, where boundaries align, From
religious doctrines to spiritual sway, Myths and
legends echo through sports' play.

In ancient times, when gods walked the earth, Sports were
offerings, to display their worth, Competitions grand, in
their divine gaze,
To honour the deities, in sacred ways.

Today, too, beliefs weave through the sports we see, A prism of
perspectives, where faith runs free,
In stadiums and arenas, a collective devotion, Where spirits
soar, in a shared emotion.

From fervent prayers, before the game's start, To rituals
performed, to invoke strength's chart, Sports become
vessels, where faith takes flight, An intertwining of bodies,
souls, and light.

In different faiths, sports find varied roles,
Uniting the faithful, igniting their souls, For
some, it's a metaphor, a spiritual quest,
A reminder of life's battles, of giving our best.

In myths and legends, too, sports are bound,
As ancient stories echo, with a resounding sound, From Hercules'

trials to Olympian might,
Their tales inspire, shining eternal light.

But let us not forget, in this complex weave, That sports are not confined, nor to one belief, For they transcend borders, cultures, and time, A universal language, where connections climb.

In today's environment, where faith intertwines, Sports become platforms, where unity aligns, Where differences dissolve, in the heat of the game, And shared values emerge, in victory's acclaim.

So, as we engage in sports' vibrant embrace, Let's honor the beliefs, the myths we chase, In respectful harmony, may our spirits align, Celebrating diversity, where connection shines.

Sport as a fine collaboration

Young and Old

In the evolution of age, where time's threads unwind, The young break records, while the elderly find, Courage to venture, on walks through town, Parks become havens, where vitality's found.

The young, with limbs of fire, push boundaries anew, In sports and games, their passions pursue,
With every leap, with every sprint,
They redefine limits, in movements mint.

But amidst the vigour of youth's boundless reign, The elderly dance, their own rhythm sustained, Through parks they wander, their steps steady and slow,
A testament to resilience, as years come and go.

Some play golf, with precision and grace, Others throw balls, a nostalgic embrace, While laughter fills the air, in carefree delight, They prove agile efforts can still shine bright.

In chair dances, their spirits take flight,
In syncopated rhythms, they find pure delight,

For age knows no bounds, no excuses to hide, Movement remains, their life's joyful tide.

For in these bodily efforts, a secret is unveiled, A key to health, a life prolonged and scaled, No matter the age, no matter the past,
Sports become pathways, where youthfulness lasts.

So let us take inspiration, from the young and the old, From records broken, to stories untold,
For in the tapestry of health and sports intertwined, We find the joy of movement, a life's vibrant sign.

No matter the age, no matter the stage, Let's embrace the call, to engage,
In sports' joyful dance, our bodies alive, Extending our life line, as we strive.

So young or old, let's heed the call, To move, to explore, to give it our all,
For in the rhythm of sports, we find the key, To a life well-lived, in spirited harmony.

Healing pain

In the sweat-drenched arena, bodies sway, Through sports' sweet alchemy, pains allay, Efforts executed, with purpose and might, Easing backaches, ailments taking flight.

As muscles engage, and movements align, A healing dance, where pains decline, Through leaps and bounds, the body heals, In sports' embrace, new strength reveals.

For health's prism is vast, it knows no bounds, From within to without, its essence resounds, With every sprint, with every throw,
A symphony of health, in each move we know.

And oh, the skin, that oft-neglected cloak, A canvas of health, where signs provoke, In sports' embrace, its brilliance untold,
A radiance emerges, a story unfolds.

As sweat purges toxins, and pores breathe free, The skin exults, in its vitality's decree,
With each regimen, a new glow bestows, A mirror of health, where beauty shows.

So let us not forget, amidst life's demands, The power of sports, in healing hands,

For in the rhythm of movements made,
A symphony of health, our bodies serenade.

Discipline is the key to success in Sport

Diet and sport

In the world of sports, where bodies transform, Diet becomes vital, a nourishing norm,
For muscles to thrive, and strength to grow, Different paths of sustenance, they must follow.

A cyclist, pedalling through winding roads, Requires fuel for endurance, a diet that bestows, Carbohydrates for energy, to power each stride, Fuelling the wheels, as they swiftly glide.

A racer, sprinting with thunderous might, Seeks explosive power, in every take-off flight,
Proteins become paramount, to rebuild and repair, Muscles fuelled, for victories to ensnare.

A bodybuilder, sculpting muscles strong,
Needs proteins in abundance, a foundation lifelong, With weights and repetitions, the body refines, Nourished by proteins, as the physique shines.

A dancer, graceful in every leap and twirl, Seeks balance and agility, a fluidity unfurl, A well-rounded diet, with nutrients diverse, Sustains the body, as movements immerse.

In the tapestry of sports, diets diverge,
Unique paths of sustenance, their bodies urge, Each discipline honing, a specific form,
With dietary adaptations, their strength takes form.

But amidst the differences, let's not forget, The common thread that binds, as a silhouette,
Health remains the essence, the guiding light, In sports and diets, harmonising in flight.

So let us nourish our bodies, with care and grace, Choosing diets aligned, with our chosen space, For in the world of sports, as bodies evolve,
Diet becomes a partner, where wellness resolves.

More on Diet and Sport

Proceeding in the world of sports, where bodies excel, Diet becomes the secret, a tale to tell,
For like horses on oats, fierce and fast they become, Feeding their fire, to rise above, overcome.

Some require wings, to soar through the sky, Running alone won't suffice, they must defy, Glucose, the fuel, for muscles in flight, Feeding the liver, a Keto fat's might.

For strategic thinking, for mental endurance, Glucose fuels the brain, a vital insurance,
In sports of strategy, where minds strategise, Diet becomes crucial, a secret to realise.

But what of those who dare to swim,
Across the English Channel, where strength is prim? For them, fat becomes their store,
Endurance is key, as they battle the shore.

In ballet's graceful realm, where elegance presides, Skinny becomes the goal, as the body glides,
Form and precision, delicate as lace,

Diet moulds the dancer, in every embrace.

In Formula One's realm, where speed takes hold, Drivers need agility, both fierce and bold,
Their bodies fine-tuned, as they race the track, Diet fuels the engine, a powerful knack.

And what of those who bear the weight,
Sumo wrestlers, mighty in their fate, With heavy strides, they claim the ring,
Diet shapes their power, as they fiercely cling.

In American football, where giants collide, Quarterbacks bear the burden, with strength beside, Burning fat into muscle, they stand tall,
Diet moulds they're physique, to take the heavy fall.

In the universe of sports, diets adapt,
From weight to endurance, each body is wrapped, For health and performance, they intertwine, Fuelling the athletes, their spirits align.

So let us honour the journey, each path's demand, Recognising the role that diets command,
In the world of sports, where bodies strive, Diet becomes a partner, in their vibrant lives.

Free diving in the wild

In the depths of the ocean, where waters run wild, A discipline emerges, both daring and beguiled, Free diving, the art of plunging deep,
Where breath becomes limited, a moment to keep.

Beneath the surface, a world unexplored, Where silence reigns, and mysteries are stored, Free divers dive, with bodies unbound, Exploring the depths, where wonders astound.

In wild waters, where currents collide,
Free divers glide, with grace as their guide, With each descent, a connection is formed,
To the vast unknown, where secrets are swarmed.

They leave the surface, shedding their breath,
Embracing the challenge, conquering death, Their bodies streamlined, in liquid embrace, Free divers surrender, with a sense of grace.

In the depths, a dance of light and shade, As they navigate, a journey self-made, With each stroke, with each gentle sway,
They explore the depths, where freedom holds sway.

The ocean becomes their sanctuary, their muse, As they delve deeper, their limits they choose, A harmony formed, between body and sea,
In free diving's realm, where spirits roam free.

But let us not forget, the risks they embrace, The dangers submerged, within this wild space, For in this discipline, where freedom abounds, Respect for the waters, a code that resounds.

In wild waters, where free divers reside,
A testament to courage, where limits are defied, They embody the spirit of the untamed,
In their depths, a passion forever ingrained.

So let us honour the free divers' plight,
Their quest for freedom, in every brave flight, For in their discipline, we witness the power, Of the human spirit, in its wildest hour.

Rodeo

In the world of grit and dust, where courage rides high, A wild symphony unfolds, beneath the vast sky,
Rodeo, the dance with horses, in wild display, And bull riding, where challengers hold sway.

From West America's plains to Argentina's land, And Brazil's vibrant spirit, a fierce band,
Nations compete, with hearts fierce and bold, In the arena of rodeo, where legends unfold.

Horses buck and whirl, their spirits untamed, As riders hold on, their dreams unashamed, A symphony of hooves, in rhythm and strife,
Man and beast entwined, in the tapestry of life.

But amidst the thrill, the danger looms near, Injuries frequent, a testament clear,
Broken bones and bruises, a warrior's mark,
A reminder of the courage that ignites in the dark.

For bull riding, a test of will and might,
As riders mount the beast, in the arena's light, Eight seconds of glory, an eternity known,

As they ride the raging bull, their fears overthrown.

Concussions and fractures, a common refrain, The toll of the sport, a price paid in pain,
Yet in the face of danger, they push beyond, Embodying resilience, their spirit responds.

For in the world of rodeo, where passion resides, The risks are embraced, where champions rise, In the thrill of the ride, they find their voice,
Unyielding and fierce, against the odds they rejoice.

So let us honour these riders, their courage untamed, In rodeo's arena, where legends are named,
For in their pursuit, they embody the heart,
Of the human spirit, where dreams find their start.

In the existence of health and sports entwined, Rodeo and bull riding, their stories defined,
A testament to the human will to dare,
To face the unknown, with resilience and compare.

King of sports 'Splash'

In the heart of local communities, a sport is crowned, A love affair with water, where health is found, Swimming, the gentle rhythm of strokes in play,
An adventure in wild waters, where souls may sway.

In neighbourhood pools, children's laughter soars, Their tiny arms flailing, as confidence restores, Learning to swim, a rite of passage, a thrill,
In the safety of waters, a sense of freedom instilled.

In tranquil lakes and rivers, where nature sings, Wild swimming awaits, with its secret springs,
A communion with the elements, an intimate blend, As bodies immerse, in water's sweet mend.

But why is swimming hailed, as the healthiest embrace? In this aqueous realm, where bodies find grace, It's the full-body workout, a symphony profound, Engaging muscles and heart, where strength is crowned.

With every stroke, a rhythm of breath and flow, Endurance blooms, as currents gently bestow,

Improving lung capacity, a gift from the deep,
In wild swimming's adventure, a promise to keep.

The waters embrace, like a mother's warm touch, Releasing tension, as worries they clutch,
Mental well-being, found in aquatic embrace, As troubles dissolve, and serenity takes place.

In the midst of local communities' thrum,
And wild swimming's allure, where spirits become, The healthiest sport crowned, in water's abode,
A celebration of life, in every fluid ode.

Embrace the power of sport

In the arena of bodies, where stress finds release, Sports emerge as a remedy, offering solace and peace.
With physical exertion, stress takes a different form, Transformed into a language the body can perform.

The weight of the world, heavy upon our hearts, Is lightened through sweat, as muscles tear apart. For in the act of movement, stress finds its voice, As bodies push boundaries, making a conscious choice.

The physical stress of sports, a paradox to find, That through the exertion, our minds are unbind. Endorphins cascade, like rivers through veins, Easing the burdens, freeing us from mental chains.

The pounding of footsteps on the ground,
Drowns out the noise, silencing thoughts profound. In the rhythm of movement, stress dissipates,
As bodies find solace, and hearts navigate.

The stress of the day, a weight to be lifted, In the arena of sports, it finds itself sifted.

With every stroke, every leap, every throw, The physical stress becomes a gift we bestow.

The body, a vessel, resilient and strong,
Absorbing stress, like a battle cry in song. As muscles ache and bones cry out,
The mind finds solace, in the midst of doubt.

In this dance of stress and release, we find, That sports can heal, a balm for the mind. Through physical exertion, a sanctuary unfurls,
As stress transforms, in the realm of twirling worlds.

So let us embrace the power of sport,
Where stress is confronted, a battle to exhort. For in the act of movement, we find our way, Reducing the stress, that burdens our day.

Chess as a Sport

In the happening of movement, a play unfolds, A juxtaposition of sports, stories yet untold.
Some demand concentration, a mind's precision, While others require raw physical provision.

Chess, the battle of wits, a sport on the board, Strategic minds dancing, victories untoward. With calculated moves, players in a trance, Mental agility showcased in each advance.

Then, the race of limbs, an athletic display, Sprinting on tracks, bodies in a swift ballet. Runners with thundering strides, muscles in flight, Physicality embodied, a captivating sight.

But what of the doubters, those who question, If these endeavours indeed meet the sport's essence?
Yet chess requires strategy, the mind's navigation, While racing demands strength, an athletic foundation.

Pondering further, let's explore the outliers, Sports that push boundaries, igniting fires.

Curling, the icebound shuffle of stones with care, Precision and teamwork, a dance to declare.

Or what of table tennis, a swift paddle in hand, The ball's rapid exchanges, a skilful command. With reflexes honed, eyes fixed on the sphere, An artistry of movement, a game played with flair.

In this interplay, the lines start to blur, As definitions shift, opinions may stir.
For what is a sport, but a passionate endeavour, Where skills and talents intertwine, forever.

So let us embrace the diversity in play,
The concentration-based and the physically inclined array.
For each sport, in its unique form and grace, Brings joy, challenges, and memories to ace.

Genetics

In the world of sports, genetics come into play, A card dealt, shaping pathways to portray.
In basketball's domain, where giants stride,
The elite skilled, towering, they take their pride.

NBA courts witness their immense stature, Dunking and soaring, a dominant capture. Their genes, a scaffold for reaching the sky, The gift of height, on which dreams rely.

But in the race tracks, a different tale unfolds, A small bodily frame, where agility moulds.
Jockeys on horses, a harmonious bond, Their stature compact, nimble, beyond.

In Formula One, the roar of engines ignite, Drivers clad in speed, adrenaline's delight. A certain physicality, an advantage held,
Quick reflexes and focus, where skill excelled.

Yet amidst the genetic tapestry we trace, Skill remains essential, the soul of the race. For even those less advantaged physically,
With mastery and prowess, they can defy decree.

In basketball's courts or race tracks' allure, The playing field equalises, skill held pure. The not-so- advantaged, they rise to the call, Their talent and dedication standing tall.

So let us celebrate the merging of genes, The diversity that shapes sporting scenes.
For in the realm of health and sports' embrace, Skill and determination leave a lasting trace.

Discipline

In the world of health and sports, a truth remains,
Discipline, the key to unlocking resilient domains. For within its embrace, happiness takes flight, And personal growth emerges, a beacon of light.

Sports, the nurturing ground where discipline thrives, Cultivating strong personas, where passion survives. Every challenge embarked upon, a flame ignites,
An action plan kindled, determination takes flight.

In the realm of martial arts, a journey unfolds, Belts climbing steadily, a story yet untold.
Persistence as the compass, continuous presence held, Years of dedication, where discipline excelled.

From the novice's white to the coveted black,
Discipline as the guide, never looking back.
Through countless hours of practice and toil, A warrior emerges, their spirit uncoil.

Driven by discipline, a statement plain and true, Yet its power and depth, only few can truly pursue.

In the discipline's grip, transformation resides, An unwavering commitment, where greatness presides.

But discipline extends beyond the sports we play, It shapes our lives in myriad ways each day.
From nutrition to routines, in habits we weave, Discipline breathes life into the goals we conceive.

So let us embrace discipline, its unwavering reign, For it builds the foundation, where dreams sustain. In health and sports, it develops the finest of souls, Igniting the path to greatness, where happiness unfolds.

Sports for all

In the world of health and sports, a call is heard, To make it accessible, for all undeterred.
For sports know no boundaries, no limits to define, Inclusive spaces where every soul can shine.

Let's witness the wonders, where disabled minds, Find solace and strength, leaving no one behind. In wheelchair basketball, a court alive with grace, Players dribbling, shooting, in a harmonious embrace.

Adaptive skiing, a dance on snowy slopes,
Where disabilities fade, replaced by endless hopes. With sit- skis and guides, gliding down the hill,
The thrill of freedom, a sensation so surreal.

Swimming, a realm where water becomes a friend, Adaptive strokes, a symphony that knows no end. Through prosthetics or limbs, in the water we fly, Weightless and buoyant, defying the sky.

And what of the unlikely, the extraordinary tales, Where limitations crumble, courage prevails?
In blind soccer, a symphony of trust and sound,

Players guided by senses, determination unbound.

Powerlifting, a stage where strength unfolds, Lifting heavy weights, defying what we're told. Adaptive equipment, levelling the playing field,
Unleashing inner power, unyielding and concealed.

Sports and disabilities, a harmonious blend, Where inclusivity and possibility transcend. Through adaptations and innovation's might, Barriers crumble, creating a radiant light.

So let us champion the cause, make sports accessible, For every person, regardless of their label.
In health and sports, let us break down the walls, And create a world where inclusion stands tall.

Hydration

For health and sports, a truth is clear,
Hydration's vital, let it always be near.
For water is the elixir, the nectar we crave,
Sustaining our bodies, like waves on a brave.

In preparation for the challenge that awaits,
Quench the body's thirst, before stepping through gates. Drink water, pure and cool, a nourishing start, Hydration's foundation, where victories impart.

During the activity, as exertion takes hold,
Hydration remains vital, like stories yet untold. Sip frequently, replenish what's lost,
For dehydration's grip is a daunting cost.

But what should we do, what should we avoid, To keep our bodies hydrated, feeling buoyed? Avoid sugary drinks, their allure may deceive, Instead, choose water, the body's reprieve.

Electrolytes, essential, they keep balance in sight, In sports drinks, they reside, a replenishing delight. But beware of excess, for moderation is key,
Too much can disrupt, a balance we decree.

In the aftermath, when the battle is done,
Hydration remains important, until the journey's run.

Replenish and restore, with water as a guide,
Reviving the body, where resilience
resides.

So let us honour the power of hydration's touch, In health and sports, its significance is such.
With each sip and gulp, we nourish and sustain, Our bodies grateful, in this vital gain.

In absolute for health and sports, hydration's the song, A symphony of wellness, where strength grows strong. So let us drink deeply, and hydrate with care,
In this fluid journey, our bodies we share.

A daily run

Sports and Ethics

In the world of health and sports, ethics hold sway, A baseline of integrity, we presume day by day.

Yet sometimes, lows befall, shadows cast their plight, But the path to redemption, a chance to make it right.

For when ethics falter, and misconduct takes hold, Recovery begins, a journey to unfold.
Apologies sincere, acknowledging the wrong,
A commitment to change, where growth becomes strong.

To compete with honour, challengers must rise, Respect and sportsmanship, where greatness lies.
For in the arena, where battles are fought, Equal treatment reigns, distinctions are naught.

No colour, no race, no gender, no label,
In sports' vibrant tapestry, we all are able.
A celebration of diversity, in every embrace,
Where the power of inclusion leaves no one in chase.

Female or male, homosexual or they,
In sports' grand symphony, they find their way. Their talents shine forth, breaking barriers, defying,
A testament to courage, where greatness lies undying.

A community united, where greatness is spread.

So let us hold the torch of ethics with care,
In health and sports, a code we must dare.

To build a world where fairness takes the stage,

And in every athlete, honour finds its gauge.

For in the dance of health and sports, we unite,
Embracing differences, in every victory's sight.
With ethics as our guide, we forge ahead,

Heroes and Legends

In the world of health and sports, legends emerge,
Heroes etched in memory, their spirits converge.
From Mohamed Ali's fists, a poetry in motion,
To Hank Bauer's feats, a hero in every notion.

Mohamed Ali, the champ of the ring,
With grace and strength, he made his swing. His words like thunder, his spirit aflame, Inspiring generations, they still chant his name.

Hank Bauer, a warrior on and off the field,

A legend in baseball, his prowess revealed. In World War II, he fought with all his might, A hero's journey, shining in wartime's light.

These icons of sport, they pave the way, Influencing young minds, inspiring each day. The power of their stories, a beacon so bright, Igniting dreams, fuelling a fearless fight.

For our young ones, they gaze in awe,
At heroes who've triumphed, against every flaw.
They dream of emulating, the greatness they see,
Becoming heroes themselves, in their own legacy.

From the rings of boxing to baseball's embrace, Our elite members, their impact we trace.
They teach us resilience, to never back down, To chase our dreams, wearing victory's crown.

So let us celebrate these heroes, near and far, Their influence transcends, like a shining star. In health and sports, their legacy prevails,

Inspiring greatness, where every dream sails.

Politics

In sports, a tangled thread,
Politics intertwines, a dance with dread.
An ugly side emerges, where power takes its toll, But in its shadow, an upside does unfold.

For politics and sport, a complex tango they share,
Where human rights falter, we must be aware.
Yet in the midst of turmoil, a glimmer of hope, Where nations unite, on a grand global scope.

The Olympics, a stage where stories intertwine, Led by Hitler, a dark chapter in history's line.
But even in that darkness, a light dared to gleam, As athletes took a stand, against hate's extreme.

Sports become a platform, a catalyst for change,

A voice for the voiceless, where courage rearrange. From Tommie Smith's raised fist, a symbol so profound, To protests against apartheid, on sacred ground.

So let us not forget, amidst politics' sway, The power of sport, to inspire and convey.
To protect human rights, and bridge nations' divide, A chance for unity, where hope shall reside.

In health and sports, a tapestry unfolds,
Where politics weaves its stories bold.
Let us learn from the past, strive for better days,
Where sports and humanity harmonise in virtuous ways.

Crazy and Entertaining

A whirlwind ensues,
Entertaining and crazy, like a carnival's muse.
From the spectacle of wrestling, fierce battles unfold, To X bull adventures, where adrenaline takes hold.

In the realm of WWE, a stage set for dreams,
Where heroes and villains engage in extreme schemes. Their bodies collide, in a choreography grand,
A performance of strength, in a fantasy land.

But in this theatre of spectacle, let us not forget,
The impact on health, the risks we must vet.
For behind the flamboyance, there lies a truth, The toll on bodies, a price paid for youth.

And in the world of adventures, adrenaline's surge, From dizzying heights to extreme acts on the verge. X bull, a catalyst for flight,
An escape from reality, a brief disconnect from sight.

But as we seek the thrills, the rush and the flare, Let us remember the balance we must declare. For health remains paramount, a guiding light, To nurture our bodies, in the pursuit of delight.
So let us revel in the entertainment and zest, But

with caution and care, let us be blessed. In health and sports, a dance we adore, Finding joy and thrill, but never ignoring more.

For in this wild happening, where reality bends, Let us capture the adventures, but make amends. To prioritise health, and find balance in the quest,

Entertaining and crazy, yet mindful, we attest.

Addiction

In the world of health and sports, a shadow lurks, Gambling's sly hand, with its dangerous quirks.

A seductive embrace, a captivating spell,
But for some, an addiction where troubles dwell.

As the thrill of the game intertwines with chance, A handicap emerges, a risky advance.
For those sensitive to addiction's haunting call, A cautionary tale, we must bravely install.

Seek not the allure of quick fortune's grasp,
But safeguard your well-being, the strength of your grasp.

Know thy limits, set boundaries in sight,
Resist the temptations, keep addiction's plight.

Find solace in sports, the beauty it brings, The joy of participation, the heart that sings. For in the sweat of effort, true fulfilment lies, A wholesome pursuit, where the spirit flies.

Surround yourself with support, a network of care,
Those who understand, who are always there.
Seek professional help, when needed in times, For recovery and healing, where hope combines.

Remember, you are not alone in this fight,
Many have faced the darkness, emerged in light. Choose health and happiness, over gambling's snare, For a life of fulfilment, beyond compare.

In health and sports, let us find our way,

A path of resilience, where addiction can't sway. With empathy and understanding, we stand, Supporting those in need, extending a hand.

So let us be vigilant, and mindful each day,
To protect our well-being, as we make our way. Therefore, let us aspire,

To foster a community, where addiction does retire.

Dope

In top sports, a shadow casts its shade, Doping's deceitful dance, a dangerous charade.
In cycling races, where endurance knows no end,
Illegal upgrades tarnish, what true skill could transcend.

The pressure mounts, the desire to excel,

To outpace the competition, their stories to tell.
But in the quest for glory, some may choose to deceive, Injecting false strength, a web they weave.

Authorities must stand firm, with a watchful eye, Ensuring athletes are advised, with respect held high. Protected by advocates who guard their mental health, Keeping them grounded, preserving inner wealth.

For the true winners emerge, not from synthetic aid,
But from perseverance and discipline, where virtues are displayed.
They honour the spirit of the sport, the body's true might, In

the pursuit of excellence, where integrity ignites.

Let us denounce the temptations, the allure of deceit,
And instead embrace the journey, where true victories meet.
In health and sports, let honesty prevail,
For in the heart of competition, truth will never fail.

So, athletes, stay centred, keep your minds aligned, Seek guidance and support, for a victory that's defined.

May your achievements be pure, your accomplishments great,
A testament to resilience, a legacy that won't abate.

Eternity

In the temple of health and sports, a secret unfurls, A key to longevity, where time gently swirls.
For as we move and exert, our cells regenerate, Slowing down the aging process, an eternal fate.

In the arena of health, a symphony of motion, Sports become the elixir, delaying life's erosion. With each breath and stride, our bodies come alive, Rejuvenating cells, like bees in a vibrant hive.

Through exercise's touch, our essence renews, Revitalizing the body, banishing aging's blues.
Muscles stretch and strengthen, bones find their might, Aging gracefully, with every move in sight.

Sport can be a dance

Carrying water home

for miles on end

Contemplating the why's and how's

The Beginning!

The Author

Sem's Bio

 After 25 years of successful investment advisory and M&A activities, delivering literally billions worth of investment capital in various ways, the time has come to proudly showcase his artistic abilities. Sem explores various forms of art, including drawings, paintings, digital art, and writings, starting with short literature books. His collection delves into the essence of maintaining good health, presented in an engaging manner, combining poetry with original digital art images.

The Secret Collection books so far written between Sem Duchateau and Heidi Schoefs

Milton Keynes UK
Ingram Content Group UK Ltd.
UKHW020038041023
429895UK00009B/69